The INSIDE GUIDE

CELEBRATING HISPANIC CULTURES

# Celebrating the People of the Dominican Republic

By Rosie Banks

Cavendish Square

New York

Published in 2023 by Cavendish Square Publishing, LLC
29 E. 21st Street New York, NY 10010



Website: cavendishsq.com



Library of Congress Cataloging-in-Publication Data

Names: Banks, Rosie, 1978- author.
Title: Celebrating the people of the Dominican Republic / Rosie Banks.
Description: New York : Cavendish Square Publishing, [2023] | Series: The inside guide: celebrating Hispanic cultures | Includes bibliographical references and index.
Identifiers: LCCN 2021040430 (print) | LCCN 2021040431 (ebook) | ISBN 9781502664662 (library binding) | ISBN 9781502664648 (paperback) | ISBN 9781502664655 (set) | ISBN 9781502664679 (ebook)
Subjects: LCSH: Dominican Republic–Juvenile literature. | Dominican Republic–Civilization–Juvenile literature.
Classification: LCC F1934.2 .B36 2023 (print) | LCC F1934.2 (ebook) | DDC 972.93–dc23
LC record available at https://lccn.loc.gov/2021040430
LC ebook record available at https://lccn.loc.gov/2021040431

Editor: Therese Shea
Copyeditor: Jill Keppeler
Designer: Deanna Paternostro

The photographs in this book are used by permission and through the courtesy of: Cover Daniele Cruciani/Shutterstock.com; p. 4 MHESIAS/Shutterstock.com; p. 6 Yakov Oskanov/Shutterstock.com; p. 8 Janusz Pienkowski/Shutterstock.com; p. 9 Roldys Jorge/Shutterstock.com; p. 10 Zoran Karapancev/Shutterstock.com; pp. 12, 29 (left) Mario De Moya F/Shutterstock.com; p. 14 Oscar Aquino/Shutterstock.com; p. 15 Brian Yarvin/Shutterstock.com; p. 16 Filippo Carlot/Shutterstock.com; p. 17 saaton/Shutterstock.com; p. 19 aleksandr paraev/Shutterstock.com; p. 20 bumihills/Shutterstock.com; p. 21 GiuseppeCrimeni/Shutterstock.com; p. 22 Rena Schild/Shutterstock.com; p. 23 BlueOrange Studio/Shutterstock.com; p. 25 Steve Edreff/Shutterstock.com; p. 27 Nikolay Antonov/Shutterstock.com; p. 28 (flag) railway fx/Shutterstock.com; p. 28 (map) Andrei Minsk/Shutterstock.com; p. 29 (center) Stefano Ember/Shutterstock.com; p. 29 (right) Lester Balajadia/Shutterstock.com.



CPSIA compliance information: Batch #CSCSQ23: For further information contact Cavendish Square Publishing LLC, New York, New York, at 1-877-980-4450.

Printed in the United States of America

# CONTENTS

The Dominican Republic takes up about two-thirds of the eastern side of the island of Hispaniola. Hispaniola is the second-largest island in the Caribbean, after Cuba.

Chapter One

# A PARADISE WITH HISTORY

The Dominican Republic is a Caribbean nation that shares the island of Hispaniola with Haiti. It's about 600 miles (966 kilometers) southeast of Florida. This **Hispanic** nation's natural beauty and its traditions—past and present—contribute to a fascinating culture.

Several groups made a home on what's now the island of Hispaniola throughout its history. The first inhabitants came on canoes from South America. When Christopher Columbus landed there in 1492, he recognized the island's value and claimed it for Spain. He called it La Isla Española (The Spanish Island). "Hispaniola" came from this name.

Before Dominican independence, control of the nation passed between Spain, France, and Haiti, so the **customs** and **ancestry** of today's Dominicans are rooted in many different backgrounds. **Indigenous** groups, Europeans, and Africans have all become part of the Dominican story.

**Fast Fact**

The Dominican Republic has the oldest continuously inhabited settlement founded by Europeans in the Western Hemisphere. Its capital, Santo Domingo, was founded in 1498.

## Indigenous Ancestors

The indigeous people of Hispaniola, the Taíno, were originally from South

America. They settled on the island around 400 BCE. A peaceful culture, they divided Hispaniola into five sections, each ruled by a cacique (chief). The Taíno people were skilled at farming and fishing. They also played a ball game called *batu* that served as a way to settle disagreements.

Historians estimate that about 3 million Taíno were on Hispaniola when the Europeans first arrived. Under Spanish rule, however, the Taíno population decreased sharply due to disease, violence, slavery,

**Most Taíno lived in huts made from palm trees. The home of the cacique was larger.**

## ENSLAVED AFRICANS ARRIVE

As the Taíno people nearly died out on Hispaniola, the Spanish looked to Africa for enslaved laborers. The first slave trade voyage known to have sailed from Africa to the Americas arrived in Santo Domingo in the early 1500s. This was the beginning of the slave trade in the Americas. If the enslaved Africans survived the horrific journey, they were put to work in the mines and sugarcane fields that made Hispaniola a wealthy colony. Slavery was outlawed in 1822, after Haiti briefly united Hispaniola. Most of today's Dominicans have a mixture of African and European ancestry.

and starvation. The remaining Taíno were forced to accept Spanish culture. Elements of the Taíno culture still survive, though. About 15 to 18 percent of Dominicans have Taíno ancestry.

**Fast Fact**

**The words "hurricane," "barbecue," "canoe," and "hammock" come from the Arawak language spoken by the Taíno.**

## Independence and Unrest

Spain **exploited** Hispaniola's people and natural resources for more than 200 years. Then, in 1697, Spain was forced to cede, or give, France the western third of Hispaniola. This region was named Saint-Domingue. In 1795, Spain ceded the remainder of the island to France. However, on the western side of the island, a revolution was being waged. Enslaved Black people

Juan Pablo Duarte is considered the father of the Dominican Republic. However, he was exiled after the revolution.

**Fast Fact**

The Mirabal sisters (*right*) were known as Las Mariposas (The Butterflies). They organized a movement against dictator Rafael Trujillo in 1959 and inspired many to fight for democracy. The sisters were killed in 1960. Trujillo was killed in 1961.

and others fought against France. They succeeded in establishing an independent state called Haiti in 1804.

In 1809, the eastern part of the island was reunited with Spain until the Spanish governor was overthrown in 1821. The people named their new nation the Independent State of Spanish Haiti. However, Haiti soon took over Spanish Haiti, controlling it for 22 years.

Juan Pablo Duarte led an effort to claim independence from Haiti and succeeded in 1844. The country was renamed after the city of Santo Domingo, but the **Republic** of Santo Domingo (now called the Dominican Republic) was far from peaceful. **Corrupt** leaders controlled the country for decades, often acting as **dictators**. In recent years, political leaders have promised **democratic** reforms.

Built from 1512 to 1541, the oldest cathedral in the Americas—the Cathedral of St. Mary of the Incarnation—is in the Dominican Republic.

# BELIEFS AND TRADITIONS

Chapter Two

Spanish **missionaries** first brought the religion of Roman Catholicism to Hispaniola. Today, about 44 percent of Dominicans are Catholic. The combining of Catholicism with folk traditions or other religions is common on the island. Some communities hold festivals to celebrate *fiestas patronales*, which are feast days for a city or town's patron saint. Patron saints are religious figures believed to offer protection and guidance. Fiestas patronales are celebrated for more than a week with music, prayers, food, and parties.

Nuestra Señora de la Altagracia (Our Lady of High Grace) is the most important religious figure in the Dominican Republic. This is a special title for Mary, the mother of Jesus Christ. Her feast day is January 21.

## Celebrations

Festivals and holidays are fun events for Dominicans. Catholic holidays include saints' feast days, Christmas, and Semana Santa, or Holy Week, which leads up to Easter.

**Fast Fact**

**For a time, the Cathedral of St. Mary of the Incarnation housed the remains of Christopher Columbus.**

Carnival performers wear elaborate costumes. Some even dress as folklore characters.

**Fast Fact**

People have been celebrating Carnival in the Dominican Republic since the early 1500s.

In January, the southeastern city of San Pedro de Macorís holds the Guloya Festival. Guloya dance groups move through the streets to the sounds of drums and flutes, celebrating the Afro-Dominican ancestry of islanders.

Taíno, African, and European traditions come together during Carnival (or Carneval). Today, Carnival takes place every Sunday in February. Dominicans celebrate with parades, costumes, music, and dancing. Cities throughout the Dominican Republic hold special events, but one of the largest occurs in the town of La Vega. In combination with Dominican Independence Day on February 27, Carnival events include military displays.

Every two years, in October, the Festival Presidente is held in Santo Domingo. It's a three-night celebration featuring the country's best performers, fireworks, and dancing.

## Cuisine

Meals have long been a part of the traditional social life in the Dominican Republic. The largest meal, at midday, is a time to relax and share food with friends or family. Dominican cooking is influenced by Spanish, African, and Taíno food. It's called *comida criolla* (**Creole** food).

Dominican recipes make use of the many foods available on and around the island. Coastal areas enjoy plentiful seafood, such as fish, conch, crab, octopus, and shrimp. Bananas and plantains are also popular and are often cooked, mashed, and mixed with other foods. Other common ingredients include rice, potatoes, yucca, cassava, and goat meat.

Unlike Mexican food, Dominican cooking generally isn't spicy but still quite flavorful. A Dominican pork stew is shown here.

## TAÍNO BREAD

The recipe for *casabe*, a flatbread usually made from cassava, started with the Taíno people. Cassava is a root vegetable that grows easily and quickly in the Caribbean. Its roots are gathered, peeled, soaked, ground, pressed, and then molded into round shapes. The Taíno cooked casabe over open fires, but most modern Dominicans use a griddle. The traditional bread can be dressed up with butter, garlic, or vegetables. It's often eaten with soup, stew, and other traditional meals. Casabe (*pictured below*) isn't fast or simple to make in the traditional way. Many feared this ancient type of bread would die out. However, people are finding ways to make it popular again.

**Fast Fact**

**Although you can make casabe with more ingredients, the Taíno often used just one—cassava.**

One classic Dominican dish is called *la bandera*, or the flag, because the colors of the dish reflect the country's flag. It's made with white rice, red beans, and meat. It's often served with salad or green plantains.

The Taíno left behind cave paintings, carvings, statues, and other artwork, such as the art shown here. Today, Dominican artists are at work all over the country, as shown on the next page.

Chapter Three

# THE ARTS

The earliest art in the Dominican Republic is in many of the island's natural caves, where Taíno people recorded their stories and beliefs. The carvings and drawings they left behind offer a glimpse into their interesting lives and creative minds. Many of these charcoal images are realistic and show how their creators looked at nature. Others are imaginative, combining animal and human figures in dreamlike ways.

Modern art in the Dominican Republic is displayed in museums, galleries, and public places. Many amateur artists sell their colorful paintings on the streets. Santo Domingo and the town of Altos de Chavón are filled with the studios of Dominican and international

**Fast Fact**
According to Taíno folklore, the first humans came from caves, which they believed were holy.

artists. The work of popular artists often illustrates and interprets life in the Dominican Republic. Art and handicrafts have become an important part of the tourist economy.

## Writers and Books

Although the Taíno expressed themselves through art and storytelling, they had no written language. Some of the first literature of what's now the Dominican Republic was written by Spanish religious leaders. The friar Bartolomé de Las Casas wrote a history of the Caribbean, including Hispaniola, in the 1500s. In his book, he urged the Spanish to act fairly toward the Taíno. Unfortunately, his advice wasn't followed.

Most Dominican authors write in Spanish, the country's official language. During the 19th century, **unique** writing styles developed that focused on life in the Dominican Republic. One famous Dominican writer was the poet Pedro Mir, often called Don Pedro. In 1993, he received the Dominican National Prize for Literature. Many people are drawn to his writings, which echo the hopes, dreams, and lives of hardworking Dominicans.

**Fast Fact**
Born in New York City but raised as a child in the Dominican Republic, Julia Alvarez is considered one of the greatest living **Latina** writers. She writes for children and adults.

## Music and Dance

Dominican culture and music are inseparable. The island's streets are

# *THE* GÜIRA

Music has a long history in the Dominican Republic. One of the instruments that has survived since the Taíno days is the *güira*. It's used to keep time in merengue and bachata songs. Listen for a rasping sound—that's the güira. The Taíno made theirs out of dried gourds. They kept the rhythm by scraping a stick along the outside of the gourd. Dominicans today have metal güiras. They use a kind of stiff brush to get the sound they want. The Dominican güira is similar to the Puerto Rican and Cuban güiro, though it has a different tone.

Dance is an important part of the identity of the Dominican Republic. Shown here are traditional Dominican dancers.

**The cities of Santo Domingo and Puerto Plata host merengue festivals. Many musicians compete for prizes.**

filled with the clear beats of merengue, but you'll also hear the longing tones of bachata and the electrifying sounds of salsa. All three musical styles provide inspiration for dancing, a favorite Dominican pastime.

**Fast Fact**

While merengue has a fast pace, bachata tends to be slower.

Merengue is the country's most popular music, played loudly and enthusiastically in many homes and public spaces. The distinctive sound of merengue developed from European and African influences and traditionally features an accordion, a type of instrument known as a güira, and a two-sided drum called a *tambora*. Merengue music is used for a kind of dance for couples that is known for its small steps and the dancers' swaying hips.

More than 65 Dominican baseball players have been selected as MLB All-Stars, including Robinson Cano, who's shown here. Others include Albert Pujols, David Ortiz, Pedro Martínez, and Miguel Tejada.

# MORE TO ADMIRE

Chapter Four

Sports are a beloved part of life in the Dominican Republic. This is especially true of baseball, which is commonly called *pelota* in this country. In the 1860s, American sailors taught the game to Cubans, who passed it on to Dominicans. As a nation, they wholeheartedly adopted the sport. There are six professional teams on the island as of 2021, and many Dominican pros also play in Major League Baseball (MLB) in the United States. These athletes have made Dominicans proud with record-breaking achievements.

Other popular sports in the Dominican Republic include volleyball and boxing. The island's beautiful beaches and inviting waters are especially suited for sailing, diving, surfing, windsurfing, and snorkeling. Hiking provides a fun way to see mountains, waterfalls, and forests. Adventurers might try white-water rafting along the island's longest river, the Río Yaque del Norte.

# FLAIR FOR FASHION

Dominicans take pride in their appearance—including their clothing. While they often wear the clothing seen in the United States and Canada, their traditional clothing was influenced by Spanish styles. For women, a traditional outfit includes a colorful long skirt or dress. Dominican men may wear a shirt called a *chacabana* with long, dark pants. (The shirt is called a guayabera in other Hispanic nations.) This lightweight shirt is typically black, white, or another light color with hand-sewn decorations. It has two or four pockets on the front and two vertical strips of fabric. The chacabana is often worn for special occasions, such as a wedding.

## Dominicans in America

Today, Dominican Americans represent a large part of the Latinx population in the United States. In the 1960s, Dominicans began to **emigrate** to the United States as a result of political problems and poverty in their nation. Most live in the Northeast, and close to half of all Dominican Americans live in New York City. Some send money from their earnings back to family they left behind.

**Fast Fact**

**Oscar de la Renta (1932–2014) was a famous fashion designer from the Dominican Republic. Celebrities around the globe have worn his creations.**

The New York City areas called Washington Heights and the Bronx are home to many Dominican residents. In fact, Washington Heights is

In New York City, the Dominican Day Parade is celebrated on the second Sunday of August.

sometimes nicknamed "Little Dominican Republic." Dominican Americans have created strong communities in which people speak Spanish and share their cultural traditions, and they have a lot to share with their fellow Americans. Their delicious dishes, energizing festivals, moving music, lively dancing, and passion for sports strengthen neighborhoods.

**Fast Fact**

More than 2 million Dominicans (or those of Dominican ancestry) lived in the United States as of 2017, a growing number. Dominicans are the fifth-largest population of Americans of Hispanic origin.

## A People to Celebrate

The history of the Dominican Republic isn't easy to understand. Power-hungry leaders throughout the country's history have mistreated Dominicans, exploited the region's natural resources, and stood in the way of peace and equality. Yet through all the troubled times, Dominicans have found a way to survive—and even thrive—by blending customs of the different peoples of the island into a rich and colorful culture. They have also rebuilt their nation into a popular vacation destination.

**Fast Fact**

Some of the main characters in the hit Broadway musical and movie *In the Heights* are Dominican. The story takes place in Washington Heights in New York City.

Today, the Dominican Republic is the most-visited destination of all the Caribbean islands. People from around the world come to Hispaniola to experience Dominicans' joyful festivals, outdoor adventures, mouthwatering meals, and cheerful merengue beats.

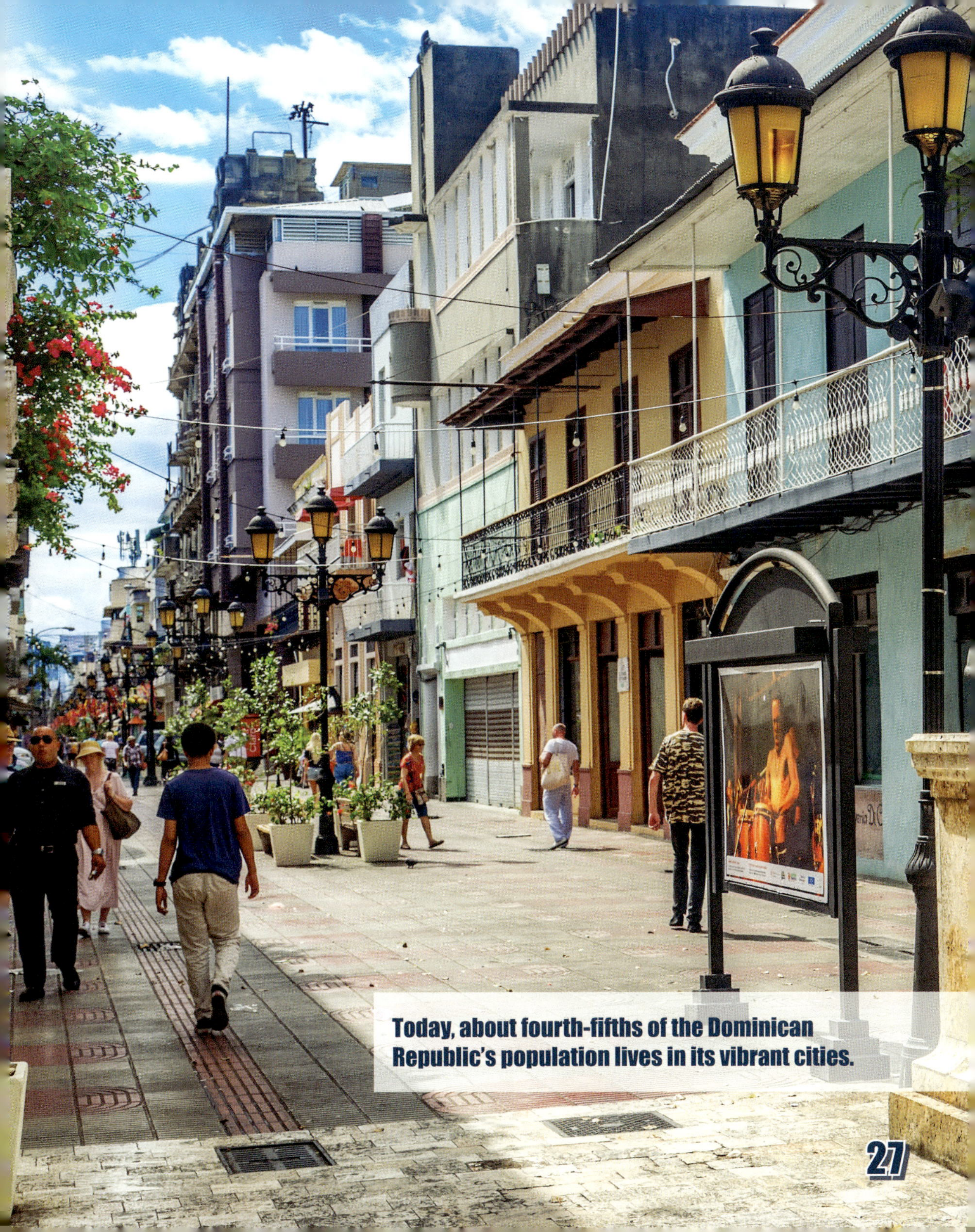

Today, about fourth-fifths of the Dominican Republic's population lives in its vibrant cities.

# NEED-TO-KNOW INFO

**Kind of Government**
presidential republic

**Population**
10,597,348 (estimate, 2021)

**Total Area**
18,792 square miles (48,670 square kilometers)

**Capital City**
Santo Domingo

**Official Country Name**
Dominican Republic (República Dominicana)

**Kind of Money**
Dominican peso

**Motto**
*Dios, patria, libertad* ("God, fatherland, liberty")

**Flag**

**Location**

# THINK ABOUT IT!

1. In what ways could the Dominican Republic honor the memory and contributions of the Taíno, past and present?
2. How do you think the Dominican Republic's political past affects Dominicans' view of government?
3. How might arts such as music and dancing strengthen Dominicans' ties to their culture?
4. Why do you think the country's popularity with tourists is both a benefit and a challenge?

# GLOSSARY

**ancestry:** The line of relatives who lived before you.

**corrupt:** Doing dishonest or illegal things to make money or gain power.

**Creole:** Referring to types of cooking and food common to Creole peoples, or those of European or African descent born in the West Indies or French or Spanish America.

**custom:** An action or way of behaving that is traditional among the people in a certain group or place.

**democratic:** Describing a form of government in which all adult citizens can participate.

**dictator:** A person who rules a country with total power, often in a cruel way.

**emigrate:** To leave a country in order to live in another.

**exploit:** To use someone or something unfairly.

**Hispanic:** Describing people who are from (or whose ancestors were from) countries where Spanish is the main language.

**indigenous:** Having to do with the first people of an area.

**Latina:** Describing a woman living in the United States whose ancestors are from Latin America. "Latino" is the male form of the word, and "Latinx" doesn't specifically refer to either gender.

**missionary:** A person sent to a country to do religious work.

**republic:** A form of government in which the people elect representatives who run the government.

**unique:** Being the only one of its kind.

# FIND OUT MORE

## Books

Orr, Tamra. *Dominican Heritage*. Ann Arbor, MI: Cherry Lake Publishing, 2018.

Rechner, Amy. *The Dominican Republic*. Minnetonka, MN: Bellwether Media, 2020.

Rogers, Barbara Radcliffe. *Dominican Republic*. New York, NY: Children's Press, 2019.

## Websites

**Dominican Republic**
*www.cia.gov/the-world-factbook/countries/dominican-republic/*
This CIA website gives a detailed account of the country.

**Dominican Republic Country Profile**
*www.bbc.com/news/world-latin-america-19246340*
This overview includes a timeline of historic events in the Dominican Republic.

**The Dominican Republic Kids Corner**
*www.domrep.org/kids.html*
Check out this page for young people hosted by the nation's embassy.

**Publisher's note to educators and parents:** Our editors have carefully reviewed these websites to ensure that they are suitable for students. Many websites change frequently, however, and we cannot guarantee that a site's future contents will continue to meet our high standards of quality and educational value. Be advised that students should be closely supervised whenever they access the internet.

# INDEX